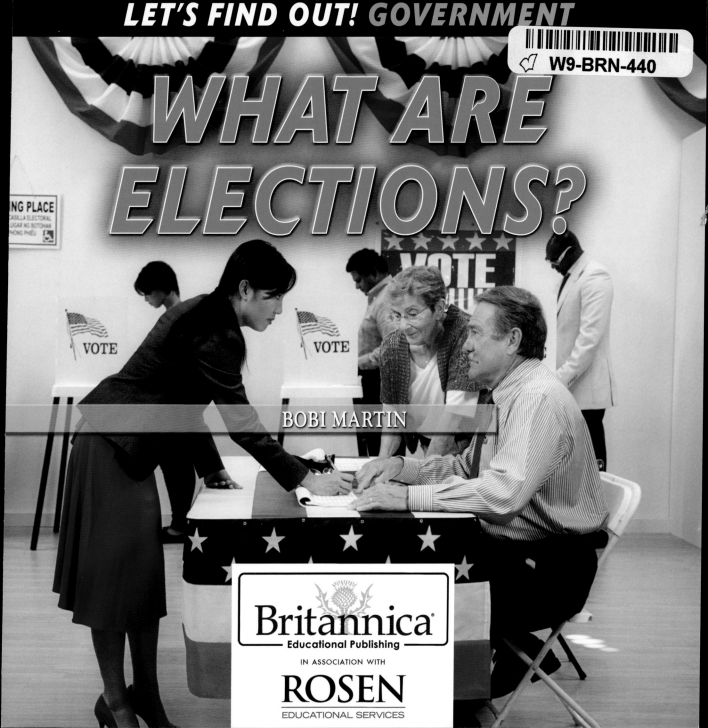

W9-BRN-440

WHAT ARE ELECTIONS?

BOBI MARTIN

Britannica®
Educational Publishing

IN ASSOCIATION WITH

ROSEN
EDUCATIONAL SERVICES

Published in 2016 by Britannica Educational Publishing (a trademark of Encyclopædia Britannica, Inc.) in association with The Rosen Publishing Group, Inc.
29 East 21st Street, New York, NY 10010

Distributed exclusively by Rosen Publishing.
To see additional Britannica Educational Publishing titles, go to rosenpublishing.com.

First Edition

Britannica Educational Publishing
J. E. Luebering: Director, Core Reference Group
Mary Rose McCudden: Editor, Britannica Student Encyclopedia

Rosen Publishing
Hope Lourie Killcoyne: Executive Editor
Shalini Saxena: Editor
Nelson Sá: Art Director
Nicole Russo: Designer
Cindy Reiman: Photography Manager

Library of Congress Cataloging-in-Publication Data

Martin, Bobi.
What are elections?/Bobi Martin.
    pages cm.—(Let's find out! government)
Includes bibliographical references and index.
ISBN 978-1-62275-966-8 (library bound)—ISBN 978-1-62275-967-5 (pbk.)—
ISBN 978-1-62275-969-9 (6-pack)
1. Elections—United States—Juvenile literature. I. Title.
JK1978.M365 2016
324.973—dc23

2014037155

Manufactured in the United States of America

Photo credits: Cover, interior pages background image Hill Street Studios/Blend Images/Getty Images; p. 4 Andy Sacks/The Image Bank/Getty Images; p. 5 skynesher/Vetta/Getty Images; p. 6 John Churchman/Photolibrary/Getty Images; p. 7 Tom Boyles/Getty Images; p. 8 Scott E. Barbour/Digital Vision/Getty Images; p. 9 Buyenlarge/Archive Photos/Getty Images; p. 10 David A. Dobbs/age fotostock/Getty Images; p. 11 Kaveh Kazemi/Hulton Archive/Getty Images; p. 12 Ulrike Welsch/Science Source/Getty Images; p. 15 (top) Comstock/Jupiterimages; pp. 15 (bottom), 23, 26 © AP Images; p. 16 Julie Denesha/Getty Images; p. 17 David McNew/Getty Images; p. 18 Visions of America/Shutterstock.com; p. 19 Archive Photos/Getty Images; p. 21 (top) Citizensharp/Wikimedia Commons/File:Iowa City Caucus.jpg/CC0; p. 21 (bottom) Mark Wilson/Getty Images; p. 22 Encyclopædia Britannica, Inc.; p. 24 Chip Somodevilla/Getty Images; p. 25 U.S. Senate, 111th Congress, Senate Photo Studio/Wikimedia Commons/File:111th US Senate class photo.jpg/CC0; p. 27 Bill Pugliano/Getty Images; p. 28 John Moore/Getty Images; p. 29 Andrea Izzotti/Shutterstock.com

CONTENTS

HAVING A VOICE

Elections are an important part of life in the United States. The Founding Fathers created a government that gave citizens the power to choose their leaders. American citizens are given the right to vote by a special document called the Constitution. Voting in elections also gives people a voice in what kind of laws they have and what kind of taxes they pay. A democracy is a kind of

Voters must sign a registration book before getting a ballot. This makes sure everyone votes only once in that election.

COMPARE AND CONTRAST

Elections give people a voice. How are elections for kids the same as elections for adults? How are they different?

Most voting is done with ballots, but students often vote by raising their hands in class or in a club.

government that allows people to have this kind of voice in how it is run.

Most elections are for adults. But kids get to vote sometimes, too. You might vote to choose the captain of your sports team. Or, perhaps your class is having a party. Your teacher says you may have hot dogs or pizza but not both. She has the class vote to decide. This is a kind of election.

WHAT IS AN ELECTION?

An election happens when a group of people votes about something, such as a new law or a new tax to raise money for schools. People also vote for leaders, like the mayor of their city or the governor of their state. The people who want these jobs are called candidates. Before an election, each candidate tries to show voters that he or she is the best person for the job. This is called campaigning. During a campaign, candidates

During a campaign, candidates tell voters what they will do if they are elected. Barack Obama campaigned before he was elected U.S. president.

THINK ABOUT IT

Many candidates give speeches during their campaign. Why is this helpful to voters?

often make speeches and put advertisements on television or on the radio.

Cities, counties, and states in the United States hold elections so people can vote for local and state issues and leaders. Every two years, elections are held so voters can choose their state's representatives in Congress. And every four years people vote for the next president.

Many voters get a sample ballot in the mail. They can mark their choices at home and bring their sample ballot when they vote.

The History of Elections

The first elections we know about were held more than 2,000 years ago in ancient Greece. The Greek elections were the first time people had a choice in their laws. The word *democracy* comes from two Greek words that mean "rule by the people."

Our government is based on democracy, but the first elections in the United States did not let all citizens have a voice. At first, only white men who owned land

The first democracy was in ancient Athens, in Greece. Democracies today are different from that one in many ways, but they also have much in common.

could vote. African American men gained the right to vote in 1870. Women also wanted a voice in elections. They made speeches and marched for suffrage. Finally, in 1920, women gained the right to vote, too. Most Native Americans were not considered citizens until 1924. After that, they could vote also. Today, most American citizens who are at least 18 years old may vote.

VOCABULARY
Suffrage means the right to vote.

Women who spoke out for the right to vote were called suffragettes. Some suffragettes were beaten or thrown into jail.

Direct Democracy or Republic?

Although the United States is a democracy, it is not a direct democracy. The Constitution says the United States is a republic. In a direct democracy, all the voters come together in one place to make laws and decisions. But often, there are too many people for a direct democracy to work. A republic is a form of democracy in which citizens elect other people to represent them

Members of the U.S. Senate and House of Representatives are elected representatives in Congress. They vote in the Capitol Building, in Washington, D.C.

COMPARE AND CONTRAST

How are a direct democracy and a republic the same? How is this form of government different from a dictatorship?

in their government. These representatives study issues and make decisions for the people who elected them. Like many countries today, the United States is a republic that practices democracy. This is also known as a representative democracy.

Some countries do not let people vote about anything. Instead, one person dictates, or makes, all the laws. Dictators rule by force. People who complain about their laws may be sent to jail! Other countries hold elections, but the government chooses who can run for office. These are not open elections because voters do not have a true choice of whom to vote for.

Dictators want to look powerful. Some dictators have huge pictures of themselves put up where citizens will see them.

GETTING REGISTERED TO VOTE

In order to vote in the United States, a person must be 18 years old and a citizen either by birth or by naturalization. A naturalized citizen is someone who was born in another country and then became an American citizen.

Most states require people to fill out a registration form before they

These people are becoming naturalized citizens. They attend a special ceremony where they pledge their allegiance to the United States.

Sometimes, volunteers set up tables near a public area to make it easier for people to register to vote.

can vote for the first time. The person must show proof of name, age, and address. In each city, a special office called the registrar makes a list of everyone who is registered to vote. At every election, voters must check off their name on the registration list before they can vote. They may also have to show a form of identification with their picture on it.

THINK ABOUT IT

A registration list helps make sure people get only one vote. What would happen if some people voted more than once in an election?

JOIN THE PARTY

Some states require voters to choose a political party when they register to vote. Political parties are groups of people who usually have similar beliefs about the role of government and how it should be run. Members of a party work together to get their leaders elected and pass laws they feel are important. When candidates run for office, their political parties will often help them with their campaigns. When voters elect members of a political party to office, the party gains more power. After an election, parties help their elected candidates try to reach that party's goals.

COMPARE AND CONTRAST
Third parties have fewer members than the main parties. But in what ways are they the same as the main parties?

The Republican Party uses an elephant as its symbol. A donkey is the political symbol of the Democratic Party.

The United States has two main parties, the Democratic Party and the Republican Party. There are many smaller parties, called third parties. Some of these are the Green Party and the Libertarian Party. Like the main parties, third parties give people a stronger voice in politics. Having more than one political party makes sure voters have a real choice.

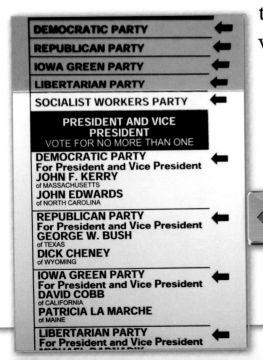

DEMOCRATIC PARTY
REPUBLICAN PARTY
IOWA GREEN PARTY
LIBERTARIAN PARTY
SOCIALIST WORKERS PARTY

PRESIDENT AND VICE PRESIDENT
VOTE FOR NO MORE THAN ONE

DEMOCRATIC PARTY
For President and Vice President
JOHN F. KERRY
of MASSACHUSETTS
JOHN EDWARDS
of NORTH CAROLINA

REPUBLICAN PARTY
For President and Vice President
GEORGE W. BUSH
of TEXAS
DICK CHENEY
of WYOMING

IOWA GREEN PARTY
For President and Vice President
DAVID COBB
of CALIFORNIA
PATRICIA LA MARCHE
of MAINE

LIBERTARIAN PARTY
For President and Vice President

Ballots list the candidates that are running for office and show which party each candidate is from.

How People Vote

Voters have an assigned polling place. It might be at a school, church, or library. At the polling place, people vote for the candidates they like or the issues, like laws or taxes, that they believe in. There are many ways to vote. Some voters use a paper ballot. To vote, they use a pen to fill in a bubble by their choice. Some voters use a machine and press a lever to make their vote.

Whether a person uses a paper ballot or votes on a computer, it is important to vote.

In other areas, computers are used. Voters make their choices by touching the computer screen.

Touch screen computers make voting easy. Voters tap the box with their choice. Then they tap another box to cast their vote.

People who will be away from home during an election may ask for an absentee ballot to be mailed to them. They can vote wherever they are and then mail their ballot to the election officials. Military personnel often use absentee ballots.

Shhh, It's a Secret!

No matter how people mark their ballot, their vote is kept a secret. Voters do not put their name on their ballot. And polling places put dividers or curtains between voters so that no one can see how someone else is voting. After people vote, their ballots are kept hidden until it is time to count them. Why is all of this important?

To keep elections fair and honest, polling places make sure no one can see how anyone else is voting.

In the past, some people used threats to make people vote a certain way. Other people offered voters money to choose the candidate that they wanted to win. Then they watched to see how people voted. This intimidated many voters. These elections were not fair or honest because people could not make their own choices. Secret voting makes sure each voter feels safe to vote the way he or she thinks is right.

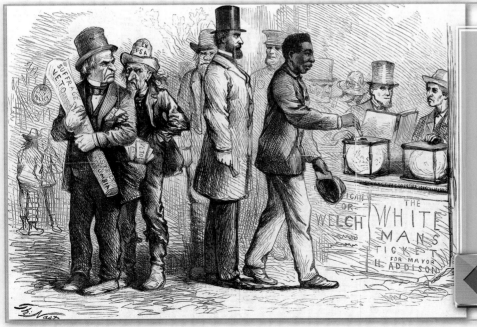

Black voters in the United States were often intimidated into not voting. The Voting Rights Act of 1965 helped to change that.

PRIMARY ELECTIONS

Many people want to run for president. But each political party may have only one candidate in the presidential election. Voters help choose the best candidate for their party. To do this, many states hold primary elections. In most primaries, citizens vote only for a candidate from their own party. Instead of primary elections, some states hold meetings called caucuses. Voters or their delegates discuss their party's candidates with other party members in their county or district. They then decide on the person they want to represent them.

COMPARE AND CONTRAST

People vote in primaries or caucuses to choose their favorite candidate. How are caucuses different from primaries?

At a caucus, people talk about the candidates and issues that are important to their state and to their party.

After the state caucuses and primary elections end, each party holds a meeting called a convention. By this time, there are usually only two or three candidates for each party. At the end of their convention, each party chooses one candidate to run for president. That candidate chooses someone to be the candidate for vice president. Both people run together as one choice on the ballot. This is called a ticket.

At the end of the 2012 Republican political convention, Mitt Romney (right) was announced as the presidential candidate and Paul Ryan was the candidate for vice president.

Who Picks the President?

In a presidential election, there is one Republican ticket and one Democratic ticket on the ballot. There may be tickets from third parties, too. Citizens vote for one of these tickets. This is called the popular vote. Usually, the ticket that wins the popular vote wins the election. But not always!

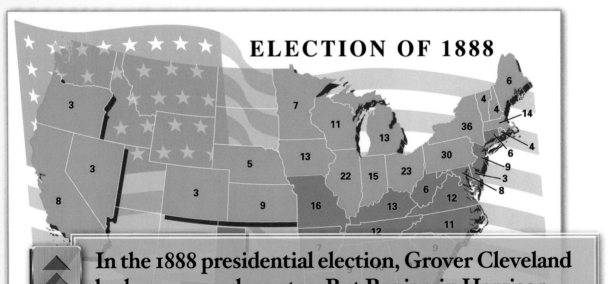

ELECTION OF 1888

In the 1888 presidential election, Grover Cleveland had more popular votes. But Benjamin Harrison had more electoral votes, so he won the election.

THINK ABOUT IT

Some people say the electoral college isn't fair. They want to go by the popular vote only. What do you think?

When voters choose one of the presidential tickets, their votes actually elect delegates in a group called the electoral college. The Founding Fathers created the electoral college to give smaller states an equal voice with larger states in choosing the president. The electoral college has 538 members. Every state has at least three delegates. States with larger populations get more delegates. The ticket with the most popular votes in a state wins all of its electoral votes. The ticket with the most electoral votes wins the election. Sometimes, the ticket with the most popular votes has fewer electoral votes, so they lose the election.

After voting ends, poll workers count the votes. When the outcome is very close, workers may have to recount the votes.

Congressional Elections

Millions of voters live in the United States. If everyone voted directly for each law or issue, it would take a long time and cost a lot of money to get anything decided. Instead, voters elect representatives from their state to vote on their behalf on laws and issues in Congress. To keep things fair, there are two houses of Congress. These are the House of Representatives, which is often just called the House, and the Senate.

Each state elects two senators to

Sometimes, both the Senate and the House of Representatives meet together. This is called a Joint Session of Congress.

Each state has two senators who serve for six years. Every two years, about one-third of the total senators run for re-election.

serve in the Senate. Voters in a state elect both senators for their state. The number of representatives a state has in the House is based on the state's population. States with more people have more representatives. States are divided into districts, and people vote only for the representative from the district they live in.

THINK ABOUT IT

Each state has two senators but a different number of representatives. Why is this fair?

SPECIAL ELECTIONS

Special elections are held when an issue must be decided before the next regular election. For example, if an elected person dies, or wants to leave office early, a special election may be held to vote for his or her replacement. If voters feel an elected person is doing a poor job, they can ask for a recall election. Then, citizens vote on whether the official must leave or may stay in office.

Recall elections are one way voters can tell elected leaders that they are not doing the job voters elected them to do.

◄◄

Citizen protests can often call attention to an issue and generate enough voter anger to spark a referendum or special election.

Elected officials use a special election, called a referendum, to ask voters to accept a special tax or to agree to a new law. Citizens can ask for a special election if they disagree with a law passed by officials. This is called an initiative. An initiative is a special election that lets voters veto a law they do not agree with.

COMPARE AND CONTRAST
Both referendums and initiatives let citizens vote on laws. How are they different?

Elect to Vote!

Voting can be hard work. Citizens must learn about the candidates so they can decide who will do the best job. They must study the issues they are voting on so they can make the right choices. Some people think this is too much work, so they do not vote. But voting in elections is an important freedom!

Elections let voters agree on the laws they live by and choose who their leaders and representatives are. Regular elections make sure elected officials do a good

Before some elections, fliers, pamphlets, or postcards may be sent out with information on the issues. They may also encourage more people to vote.

job. If voters don't like the job an official does, they can choose a new candidate in the next election. Voting makes sure the voice of the people is heard. It keeps leaders working for the people and the issues that are important to them. Without voters, a democracy would not survive.

THINK ABOUT IT

In some countries, everyone *must* vote. People who don't vote may pay a fine. Do you think this is a good idea? Why or why not?

Whether you vote for the next president of the country or of your class, voting is an important duty that can help make a difference.

GLOSSARY

absentee ballot A ballot sent by mail because the voter cannot vote in the polling place on election day.

ballot The form voters use to mark their choices.

caucus A meeting held instead of a primary to choose a state's candidate for each political party.

Congress The two groups, or houses, that represent voters in the national government.

Constitution The document that defines the rules for the U.S. government.

convention A large gathering in which a political party chooses its final candidate for president.

delegate A person who speaks or votes for other voters.

dictator A ruler who is not elected to office and who governs by force.

electoral college The group of delegates from each state that actually elects the president.

Founding Fathers The men who created the Constitution. Also, the men who signed the Declaration of Independence.

initiative A special election called for by voters to approve or veto a law.

military personnel People who belong to the air force, navy, or other branch of service.

political parties Groups of people with similar ideas who work together.

primary election An election held by some states so voters can choose each party's presidential candidate.

referendum A special election held by officials so citizens can vote on a tax or law.

registrar The office that keeps voter registration forms and lists.

represent To act on behalf of someone else.

representative democracy A form of government in which citizens vote for other people to represent them.

ticket A list of candidates for election; usually candidates for president and vice president who are listed together on the ballot as one choice.

FOR MORE INFORMATION

Books

Baicker, Karen. *The Election Activity Book: Dozens of Activities That Help Kids Learn About Voting...and More.* New York, NY: Scholastic, Inc., 2012.

Benoit, Peter. *Women's Right to Vote.* Danbury, CT: Children's Press, 2014.

De Capua, Sarah. *Voting.* New York, NY: Children's Press, 2013.

Friedman, Mark. *The Democratic Process.* Danbury, CT: Children's Press, 2012.

Gagne, Tammy. *A Kid's Guide to the Voting Process* (Votes America). Hockessin, DE: Mitchell Lane Publishers, 2012.

Websites

Because of the changing nature of Internet links, Rosen Publishing has developed an online list of websites related to the subject of this book. This site is updated regularly. Please use this link to access the list:

http://www.rosenlinks.com/LFO/Elect

Index